Encounters with God

The Gospel of MARK

Encounters with God Study Guide Series

The Gospel of Matthew
The Gospel of Mark
The Gospel of Luke
The Gospel of John
The Acts of the Apostles
The Book of Romans

Encounters with God

The Gospel of MARK

Henry Blackaby, Th.M., D.D.
Richard Blackaby, M.Div., Ph.D.
Thomas Blackaby, M.Div., D.Min.
Melvin Blackaby, M.Div., Ph.D.
Norman Blackaby, M.Div., B.L., Ph.D.

Published by Thomas Nelson, Inc., P.O. Box 141000, Nashville, Tennessee 37214.

Library of Congress Cataloging-in-Publication Data
ISBN 1-4185-26398 9781418526399

Printed in the United States of America

07 08 09 10 RRD 9 8 7 6 5 4 3 2 1

Contents

An Introduction to the Gospel of Mark 7

An Overview of Our Study of the Gospel of Mark 11

The Lessons:

Lesson #1: Jesus Delivers from Unclean Spirits 15

Lesson #2: Jesus Forgives and Heals 27

Lesson #3: Jesus Commands Nature 39

Lesson #4: Jesus Raises the Dead 49

Lesson #5: Jesus Multiplies Bread and Fish 59

Lesson #6: Jesus Confronts His Opposition 69

Lesson #7: Jesus Dies and Rises from Death 79

Notes to Leaders of Small Groups 87

An Introduction to the Gospel of Mark

The Gospel of Mark is the second book of the New Testament. It was written primarily for Gentiles (non-Jewish people) and especially for Roman believers. From the beginning, this book has been uniquely associated with Rome, where a sizable Christian community was located. Mark may have been the earliest of the four Gospels, since Matthew and Luke seem to have drawn extensively from its material.

A Gospel Account. Mark is a Gospel account—one of four books in the New Testament labeled *Gospels*. It joins Matthew, Luke, and John as a book that focuses on Jesus—what He did, what He said, and who He was and is. The word *gospel* literally means *good news*. The good news for Mark was bound up primarily in the life, death and resurrection of Jesus Christ. Essentially evangelistic in nature, the events and teachings Mark presented culminate in the cross and empty tomb. The truth that Jesus suffered, died, and rose again was a message of tremendous hope to the Romans, who experienced a great deal of persecution and martyrdom for their faith.

A Synoptic Gospel. Mark is one of the three *synoptic* Gospels, along with Matthew and Luke. The word *synoptic* means *seeing from one viewpoint* or *one overview*. Mark, Matthew, and Luke cover many of the same incidents and messages of Jesus in their Gospel accounts. In many ways, their presentations are similar to three photograph albums taken by three different photographers covering essentially the same life and events. Just as each photographer has a unique vantage point, angle, and composition, so each of the synoptic Gospels has a distinct voice, style, and purpose. Each Gospel has a tone, pace, and emphasis that is unique.

Perhaps the foremost word to describe the Gospel of Mark is *action*. No effort is wasted. No time is spent on the frivolous. More than any other New Testament book, the Gospel of Mark uses the word *immediately* (sometimes translated *straightway*) and many of the verbs are in the present tense. The pace is fast, the language vivid, and in many cases, the Gospel of Mark presents in only a few verses what other writers describe in greater depth. It is the shortest of the four Gospels, and while other accounts deal in more expansive ways with Jesus' birth or divine origin, Mark focuses tightly on Jesus' ministry, chronicling His actions without feeling a need to see them as a fulfillment of prophecy (as Matthew did).

From many different angles, Mark tells of Jesus' *power*. Jesus has authority over all manner of sickness, disease, and ailment. He has power over unclean spirits, natural law, and death. He confronts His opposition directly, both in the natural and spiritual realms. In the end, He lays down His own life and rises from the dead. Rome—which ruled with power—and Romans, who admired power—are challenged to see Jesus as bearing supreme and eternal power.

While dealing primarily with the deeds of Jesus, Mark is also the Gospel writer who describes most the emotions of Jesus. Jesus is not an unfeeling, uncaring, untouchable Savior and Lord—He is the opposite of the *uninvolved* Roman deities. Mark speaks repeatedly about Jesus' compassion, love, joy, anger, wonder, awe, grief, distress, and sorrow. Jesus not only teaches, but He touches even those considered ritually or religiously unclean. Jesus rebukes those who attempt to thwart His purpose, embraces little children and blesses them, and [not in this book] challenges those who fail to believe Him. Jesus fully expresses the power of the incarnation—God's Spirit wrapped in human flesh.

Mark the Author. Mark was not one of the original twelve disciples, but he did witness much of what happened in the early church and he appears to have known and heard Jesus. Some believe the Last Supper was held in the home of Mark's mother, and that Mark identified himself in writing as a young man wearing only a linen cloth in the Garden of Gethsemane (Mark 14:51–52). Early church prayer meetings appear to have been held in his home (Acts 12:12).

Early Christian writings leave little doubt that his name was John (Hebrew) Mark (Roman), the son of Mary and a kinsman of Barnabas. Paul refers to him as a cousin of Barnabas (Colossians 4:10). John Mark traveled with Paul and Barnabas (Acts 13:5, 13). He also spent much time with Peter, one of the original twelve disciples, who referred to Mark as *my son*, a reference to their close spiritual bond. (See 1 Peter 5:13.) Peter certainly was one of the disciples closest to Jesus and a man known for action. The same was true for Paul. Mark, in his youthfulness, may naturally have gravitated to these men as his role models, and have been eager for a faith adventure that extended far beyond his home in Jerusalem. A young man on the move, Mark reveals to us the action-packed, miracle-packed ministry of Jesus.

Mark, a Jew, gave some explanation to his readers about Jewish customs and Aramaic words or phrases (Mark 7:2–4; Mark 3:17; 5:41, respectively). His purpose, however, was not to convince his readers of Jesus' qualifications as the Jewish Messiah as much as it was to present Jesus as the Christ for all who would believe in Him. For this reason, many new Christians today find Mark the most accessible of the four Gospels in gaining a sweeping-overview understanding of what Jesus did and said.

An Overview of Our Study of the Gospel of Mark

This study guide presents seven lessons drawn from and based largely on the Gospel of Mark. The study guide elaborates on, and is based on, the commentary included in the *Blackaby Study Bible*. The lessons are arranged in the order they appear in Mark's Gospel—which is a chronological presentation of the ministry of Jesus:

Lesson #1: Jesus Delivers from Unclean Spirits

Lesson #2: Jesus Forgives and Heals

Lesson #3: Jesus Commands Nature

Lesson #4: Jesus Raises the Dead

Lesson #5: Jesus Multiplies Bread and Fish

Lesson #6: Jesus Confronts His Opposition

Lesson #7: Jesus Dies and Rises from Death

Personal or Group Use. These lessons are offered for personal study and reflection or for small-group Bible study. The questions may be answered by an individual reader or used as a foundation for group discussion. A section titled "Notes to Leaders of Small Groups" is included at the back of this book to help those who lead a small-group study of the material.

Before you embark on this study, we encourage you to read in full the article in the *Blackaby Study Bible* entitled "How to Study the Bible" on pages viii–ix. The Bible is unique among all literature. It is God's definitive word for humanity. The Bible is

- *inspired*—God breathed
- *authoritative*—absolutely the final word on any spiritual matter
- *the plumb line of truth*—the standard against which all human activity and reasoning must be evaluated

The Bible is fascinating in that it has remarkable diversity, but also remarkable unity. The books were penned by a diverse assortment of authors representing a variety of languages and cultures. The Bible as a whole has a number of literary forms. But, the Bible's message from cover to cover is clear, consistent, and unified.

More than mere words on a page, the Bible is an encounter with God Himself. No book is more critical to your life. The essence of the Bible is the Lord Himself.

God speaks by the Holy Spirit through the Bible. He also communicates during your time of prayer, in your life circumstances, and through the church. Read your Bible in an attitude of prayer and allow the Holy Spirit to make you aware of God's activity in and through your personal life. Write down what you learn, meditate on it, and adjust your thoughts, attitudes, and behavior accordingly. Look for ways every day in which the truth of God's Word can be applied to your circumstances and relationships. God is not random, but orderly and intentional in the way He speaks to you.

Be encouraged—the Bible is *not* too difficult for the average person to understand if that person asks the Holy Spirit for help. (Furthermore, not even the most brilliant person can fully understand the Bible apart from the Holy Spirit's help!) God desires for you to know Him and His Word. Everyone who reads the Bible can learn from it. The person who will receive maximum benefit from reading and studying the Bible, however, is the one who:

- *is born again* (John 3:3, 5). Those who are born again and have received the gift of God's Spirit have a distinct advantage in understanding the truths of His Word.
- *has a heart that desires to learn God's truth*. Your attitude greatly influences the outcome of Bible study. Resist the temptation to focus on what others have said about the Bible. Allow the Holy Spirit to guide you as you study God's Word for yourself.
- *has a heart that seeks to obey God*. The Holy Spirit teaches most those who have a desire to apply what they learn. Begin your Bible study with prayer, asking the Holy Spirit to guide your thoughts and to impress upon you what is on God's heart. Then, make plans to adjust your life immediately to obey the Lord fully.

As you read and study the Bible, your purpose is not to *create* meaning, but to *discover* the meaning of the text with the Holy Spirit's guidance. Ask yourself, "What did the author have in mind? How was this applied by those who first heard these words?" Especially in your study of the Gospel accounts, pay attention to the words of Jesus that begin "Most assuredly" or "He opened His mouth and taught them, saying." These are core principles and teachings that powerfully impact every person's life.

At times you may find it helpful to consult other passages of the Bible (made available in the center columns in the *Blackaby Study Bible*) or the commentary in the margins of the *Blackaby Study Bible.*

Always keep in mind that Bible study is not primarily an exercise for acquiring information, but it is an opportunity for personal transformation. Bible study is your opportunity to encounter God and to be changed in His presence. When God speaks to your heart, nothing remains the same. Jesus said, "He who has ears to hear, let him hear" (Matthew 13:9). Choose to have ears that desire to hear!

The B-A-S-I-Cs of Each Study in This Guide. Each lesson in this study guide has five segments, using the word BASIC as an acronym. The word BASIC does not allude to elementary or simple, but rather to *foundational.* These studies extend the concepts that are part of the *Blackaby Study Bible* commentary and are focused on key aspects of what it means to be a Christ-follower in today's world. The BASIC acronym stands for:

B = *Bible Focus.* This segment presents the central passage for the lesson and a general explanation that covers the central theme or concern.

A = *Application for Today.* This segment has a story or illustration related to modern times, with questions that link the Bible text to today's issues, problems, and concerns.

S = *Supplementary Scriptures to Consider.* In this segment, other Bible verses related to the general theme of the lesson are explored.

I = *Introspection and Implications.* In this segment, questions are asked that lead to deeper reflection about one's personal faith journey and life experiences.

C = *Communicating the Good News.* This segment presents challenging questions aimed at ways in which the truth of the lesson might be lived out and shared with others (either to bring salvation to others or to build up believers).

Lesson #1

JESUS DELIVERS FROM UNCLEAN SPIRITS

Unclean spirits: powerful evil forces that cause a person to act in a wicked manner apart from that person's will.

B
Bible Focus

Then they went into Capernaum, and immediately on the Sabbath He entered the synagogue and taught. And they were astonished at His teaching, for He taught them as one having authority, and not as the scribes.

Now there was a man in their synagogue with an unclean spirit. And he cried out, saying, "Let us alone! What have we to do with You, Jesus of Nazareth? Did You come to destroy us? I know who You are—the Holy One of God!"

But Jesus rebuked him, saying, "Be quiet, and come out of him!" And when the unclean spirit had convulsed him and cried out with a loud voice, he came out of him. Then they were all amazed, so that they questioned among themselves, saying, "What is this? What new doctrine is this? For with authority He commands even the unclean spirits, and they obey Him." And immediately His fame spread throughout all the region around Galilee (Mark 1:21–28).

Mark opens his Gospel as if bursting from a gated chute. In twenty short verses he covers the ministry of John the Baptist, Jesus' baptism by John in the Jordan River, the temptation of Jesus in the wilderness, the earliest preaching message of Jesus, and the call of four fishermen to be disciples. The message of Jesus in the earliest days of His earthly ministry is summarized by Mark in eighteen words, "The time is fulfilled, and the kingdom of God is at hand. Repent, and believe in the gospel" (Mark 1:15).

Then, Mark launches into the first supernatural act of Jesus' ministry—the casting out of an unclean spirit. Mark very quickly establishes that Jesus had authority over unclean spirits—they obeyed His commands fully and definitively.

Jesus performed this act of deliverance in public view. He was in a synagogue in Capernaum, the city Jesus seems to have adopted as His ministry headquarters. As was customary for rabbis and those who were well-known teachers, Jesus was given the privilege of teaching. Those who heard Him described Him as teaching with authority to the point they were astonished. Then, apparently in response to Jesus' teaching, a man with an unclean spirit cried out uncontrollably. In torment, the demons demanded to be left alone. They clearly knew who Jesus was, the *Holy One of God*.

Rather than leave the unclean spirits alone, Jesus confronted them and commanded that they leave the man they had inhabited. His command was simple and direct: "Be quiet, and come out of him" (Mark 1:25). The unclean spirits convulsed the man but apparently did not utter a sound . . . and they left. Jesus both taught and then acted with healing, delivering power in a manner that left the people stunned in awe.

Do demons exist? Are they active today? If so, how are we to deal with them?

Believers have asked these questions through the centuries, and they continue to be asked by believers around the world today.

Demonic power is alluded to in the Old Testament, but there are no examples of demonic possession and deliverance from being possessed. Nevertheless, Jewish people from the earliest times recognized that the devil existed and that he had power to entice people to disobey God's commands and to speak and act wickedly. The devil is characterized throughout Scripture as having access to a person's mind, with the intent of prompting willful acts that defy God and seek to countermand His authority over all things.

Demons are traditionally defined as evil spirits that seek to express themselves through living creatures. They are presented throughout the New Testament as being personable and intelligent (Acts 16:16–18), having supernatural strength (Luke 8:29; Acts 19:13–16), and being fully aware that Jesus is divine. They torment their victims and work in direct opposition to God's work with varying levels of influence, oppression, and possession. They can cause both physical torment and mental anguish. They do *not* possess believers.

Demons appear to have been particularly active at the time of Jesus, perhaps because they knew their days were numbered and their power was subject to limitation. With the incarnation of the Son of God, the realm of evil spirits was being invaded and conquered.

A significant segment of the population in Western cultures today does not believe demons exist. Scoffers cite various mental illnesses and physical illnesses as having tormenting power. Jesus, however, called unclean spirits for what they were: He knew them to be rebellious spirits against God, in league with Satan. These spirits knew Jesus to be the Holy One of God.

Jesus did not teach about demons, but whenever He was confronted by evil, He banished it from His presence and from the lives of people sorely afflicted by its controlling impulses. His purpose was not to seek out sickness or evil spirits. He also did not want to grandstand or astonish His audiences with His supernatural power. Rather, Jesus sought to set people free from whatever it was that placed them in bondage (John 8:32). He wanted to remove any obstacle that might arise that caused people to become distracted or confused about the truth of who He was and what He taught.

Perhaps the most potent form of human power identified and admired in the ancient world was spiritual power. Mark begins his Gospel with a clear statement that Jesus had spiritual power that was divine.

How do you explain terrible acts of wickedness in our world today?

What do you believe to be the role of Christians in confronting evil? How do we cast out evil wherever and whenever we encounter it?

A
Application for Today

A man walked into a large downtown church. He was dirty and unkempt, obviously one of the inner-city street people who were routinely offered a sandwich and cup of coffee in a church-operated ministry half a block away from the cathedral.

The man made his way to the front pew and sat down. During the song service, he waved his arms as if conducting a choir, and when the choir began to sing, he became even more animated in his conducting. Tension filled the air, as parishioners began to look at one another wide-eyed and somewhat alarmed. Was the man dangerous or just deranged? Should something be done, or should he be left alone? Was he sober or drunk? Was it acceptable to smile at his behavior, or was it better to wear a furrowed brow and a frown? Was he a paid actor, or a real street person?

When the time came for the parishioners to approach the altar to partake of Communion, the man joined those in line to receive the elements. When offered a wafer as the "Body of Christ," he gobbled it eagerly and announced in a loud voice, "That has no taste!" When the chalice of wine was extended to him as the "Blood of Christ, the cup of salvation," he gulped the entire contents of the chalice and stood to announce, "That was no blood and the Blood of Christ doesn't mean anything anyway." He launched into a tirade of obscenities and vulgarities, all of which seemed aimed at denouncing not only the church, but Jesus as the Savior.

Ushers quickly moved in to escort the man from the building. He did not go calmly, but kicked and screamed in a manner that required four men to eventually lift him bodily and carry him out to the street, where they waited with him until an ambulance arrived.

At a meeting with the ushers the following week, the advice was given: "Act sooner rather than later." However, no one could define when *sooner* might be.

What should have been done in this case? And when?

It's one thing to look back on an incident and map a strategy. It's another to state what others should have done, and why. What would *you* have done had you been a member of that church and in attendance that Sunday morning? Would it have made a difference if you had been a person in a leadership position, such as an usher or board member or a member of the pastoral staff?

How would you have determined if such a person was mentally deranged or spiritually wicked? Would it have made a difference in your response to him?

S

Supplementary Scriptures to Consider

Jesus' deliverance of people from evil spirits was apparently not an uncommon event. Jesus' popularity grew very quickly after this first incident identified in the Gospel of Mark, and we read just a few verses later:

> Now in the morning, having risen a long while before daylight, He went out and departed to a solitary place; and there He prayed. And Simon and those who were with Him searched for Him. When they found Him, they said to Him, "Everyone is looking for You."
>
> But He said to them, "Let us go into the next towns, that I may preach there also, because for this purpose I have come forth."
>
> And He was preaching in their synagogues throughout all Galilee, and casting out demons (Mark 1:35–39).

- Often in today's world, prayer for the healing of physical and spiritual ailments takes place in non-church settings or in more private settings—special rallies, meetings, seminars, or at side altars. How would the people in the Galilean synagogues respond to having demons cast out of those in attendance? What about today?

- Consider this statement: "Demons are active only when the gospel is being proclaimed with authority and Jesus Christ is being lifted up as sovereign God." Do you agree or disagree? Why or why not?

One of the foremost examples of a demon-possessed man being healed is that of a man who lived on the eastern side of the Sea of Galilee:

> Then they came to the other side of the sea, to the country of the Gadarenes. And when He had come out of the boat, immediately there met Him out of the tombs a man with an unclean spirit, who had his dwelling among the tombs; and no one could bind him, not even with chains, because he had often been bound with shackles and chains. And the chains had been pulled apart by him and the shackles broken in pieces; neither could anyone tame him. And always, night and day, he was in the mountains in the tombs, crying out and cutting himself with stones.
>
> When he saw Jesus from afar, he ran and worshiped Him. And he cried out with a loud voice and said, "What have I to do with You, Jesus, Son of the Most High God? I implore You by God that You do not torment me."
>
> For He said to him, "Come out of the man, unclean spirit!" Then He asked him, "What is your name?"
>
> And he answered, saying, "My name is Legion; for we are many." Also he begged Him earnestly that He would not send them out of the country.
>
> Now a large herd of swine was feeding there near the mountains. So all the demons begged Him, saying, "Send us to the swine, that we may enter them." And at once Jesus

gave them permission. Then the unclean spirits went out and entered the swine (there were about two thousand); and the herd ran violently down the steep place into the sea, and drowned in the sea.

So those who fed the swine fled, and they told it in the city and in the county. And they went out to see what it was that had happened. Then they came to Jesus, and saw the one who had been demon-possessed and had the legion, sitting and clothed and in his right mind. And they were afraid. And those who saw it told them how it happened to him who had been demon-possessed, and about the swine. Then they began to plead with Him to depart from their region.

And when He got into the boat, he who had been demon-possessed begged Him that he might be with Him. However, Jesus did not permit him, but said to him, "Go home to your friends, and tell them what great things the Lord has done for you, and how He has had compassion on you." And he departed and began to proclaim in Decapolis all that Jesus had done for him; and all marveled" (Mark 5:1–20).

- Swine were not only considered unclean animals, they were appropriately kept at the city dump and allowed to roam cemeteries. Swine were also animals routinely offered as sacrifices to the god below as part of Roman rituals. Rome ruled the ten cities of Decapolis, and the Roman gods were routinely worshiped there. The swine possessed by devils were destined for sacrifice. Jesus simply speeded up the process of their death! Mark wrote that the people of the area pleaded with Jesus to depart from their region. Why? Would you have asked that He leave your town? Your field?

- This man's deliverance was immediate and complete. He was able to sit calmly, remain clothed, and speak in his right mind. These attributes are hallmarks of mental health: an ability to focus, to adhere to cultural and social normative behavior, and to speak rationally. How comfortable are you in the presence of people who are mentally ill? How are qualities associated with mental health impacted by too much stress?

- Jesus sent this man home to his friends to tell them what had happened and to express the compassion of the Lord. Is it more or less difficult to witness about Christ Jesus to those who know you well and have seen you at your worst?

The opponents of Jesus attempted to explain His supernatural power over evil spirits by claiming He was in league with them:

> The scribes who came down from Jerusalem said, "He has Beelzebub," and, "By the ruler of the demons He casts out demons."
>
> So He called them to Himself and said to them in parables: "How can Satan cast out Satan? If a kingdom is divided against itself, that kingdom cannot stand. And if a house is divided against itself, that house cannot stand. And if Satan has risen up against himself, and is divided, he cannot stand, but has an end. No one can enter a strong man's house and plunder his goods, unless he first binds the strong man. And then he will plunder his house" (Mark 3:22–27).

Can you cite an example of this truth that a kingdom or house divided against itself cannot stand, but it has an end?

- Reflect on this statement, "No one can enter a strong man's house and plunder his goods, unless he first binds the strong man." What implications does this statement have for the role of intercessory prayer in evangelism, healing, or deliverance from evil?

Jesus was misunderstood even by His own family:

> "But when His own people heard about this, they went out to lay hold of Him, for they said, "He is out of His mind" (Mark 3:21).

When Jesus' own family members and friends heard about the crowds He was attracting and the deliverance miracles He was performing, they questioned His sanity. Have people you dearly loved ever questioned your sanity or stability after you accepted Jesus Christ as your Savior or you sought to obey what Jesus was telling you to do? How did you respond? What were the results?

I
Introspection and Implications

1. What do you think when you hear the word "*demonic*"? Are you curious about demons? Do you dismiss the notion that demons exist? Do you believe they exist and pray you never encounter one? Do you suspect demons might be at work in a particular person's life but don't want to say anything because you fear what others might think of you?

2. How do you *"feel"* about the possibility of demonic activity or influence in the world around you? What is your emotional response to evil or unclean spirits? Do you feel fear? Dread? Anxiety?

3. Is it ever the "right thing" to "do nothing" for a person you believe is suffering with mental, emotional, or spiritual problems?

4. How do you define and differentiate among the spiritual conditions listed below?
   - Spiritual impression to do evil
   - Spiritual oppression (or spiritual depression)
   - Spiritual possession

   How should we respond to each of the above when we encounter it?

C
Communicating the Good News

There is no mention in Scripture that those who truly acknowledge Jesus as Savior and are following Him as their Lord can be or are spiritually *possessed*. A believer might be discouraged in spirit, even feel depressed or oppressed, but a believer is not *possessed*. What would you say to a person who confided in you that he or she felt surrounded by spiritual darkness? What would you say to a person who said, "I cannot help myself. The devil makes me do what I do"?

Mark concluded his Gospel with this command from Jesus to His disciples:

> "Go into all the world and preach the gospel to every creature. He who believes and is baptized will be saved; but he

> who does not believe will be condemned. And these signs will follow those who believe: In My name they will cast out demons; they will speak with new tongues; they will take up serpents; and if they drink anything deadly, it will by no means hurt them; for they will lay hands on the sick, and they will recover" (Mark 16:15–18).

In what ways are we capable of manifesting, and authorized to manifest, these signs Jesus said would follow those who believe? Are we ever wise to seek out opportunities to do these things or is it better to focus on preaching the gospel and dealing with these things as they may or may not arise?

Mark gives this summary statement about what Jesus' disciples did after He ascended into heaven:

> And they went out and preached everywhere, the Lord working with them and confirming the word through the accompanying signs (Mark 16:20).

In what ways do miraculous signs confirm the truth of the gospel to unbelievers? Encourage believers? Confuse both unbelievers and believers?

Lesson #2

JESUS FORGIVES AND HEALS

Wholeness: the whole of a person's being. Jesus did not segment or divide a human being. The root word in Hebrew is the same for salvation and healing. A person is not truly whole unless he is made well in spirit, mind, emotions, and body with all aspects of his being functioning in harmony and unity.

B
Bible Focus

And again He entered Capernaum after some days, and it was heard that He was in the house. Immediately many gathered together, so that there was no longer room to receive them, not even near the door. And He preached the word to them. Then they came to Him, bringing a paralytic who was carried by four men. And when they could not come near him because of the crowd, they uncovered the roof where He was. So when they had broken through, they let down the bed on which the paralytic was lying.

When Jesus saw their faith, He said to the paralytic, "Son, your sins are forgiven you."

And some of the scribes were sitting there and reasoning in their hearts, "Why does this Man speak blasphemies like this? Who can forgive sins but God alone?"

But immediately, when Jesus perceived in His spirit that they reasoned thus within themselves, He said to them, "Why do you reason about these things in your hearts? Which is easier, to say to the paralytic, 'Your sins are forgiven you,' or to say, 'Arise, take up your bed and walk'? But that you may know that the Son of Man has power on earth to forgive sins"—He said to the paralytic, "I say to you, arise, take up your bed, and go to your house." Immediately he arose, took up the bed, and went out in the presence of them all, so that all were amazed and glorified God, saying, "We never saw anything like this!" (Mark 2:1–12)

We tend to segment human beings. We refer to a person's emotions, thoughts, and will as though a person can think without having an accompanying emotion or impulse to act (even if the action is to think a second thought).

We refer to a person's body as if it has a capability of functioning independently of that person's emotions, mind, or spirit.

People in the time and culture of Jesus did not divide the human being. They routinely saw sin and sickness as being linked. The common diagnosis for the man who was paralyzed likely was that he had sinned grievously and his inability to move was related to his guilt and shame. Healing, of course, was virtually impossible for such a person who had sinned to that degree—there was no absolution for such profound guilt.

Mark wrote that Jesus saw the *faith* of the men who brought this man to him. What an extraordinary effort they had made. Seeing that the house was packed with people, they had made their way up the outer staircase to the home's flat roof and there they had taken apart the tiles and earth used to make the ceiling above where Jesus was teaching. They lowered their friend directly into Jesus' presence. Jesus immediately recognized these men *believed* their friend could and should be set free from his paralysis. In other words, from their perspective, whatever had caused this man to become immobile was reversible. He also saw they were placing full confidence and trust in Him to do what no other human being could do. Jesus responded to their faith.

Very often people believe Jesus heals on the basis of the severity of a need. That is not the New Testament pattern. Jesus responds primarily to expressions of faith.

Do you have faith to believe the condition of someone you know is reversible? How important is it to have such faith when you pray for that person or take that person to a place where they might be helped?

Jesus first pronounced forgiveness to the paralyzed man. He referred to him with a personal and affectionate term: "Son" (Mark 2:5).

The actions of Jesus immediately evoked strong reaction in His critics who were present. Jesus could read their thoughts and He responded, "Which is more difficult? To forgive sin or heal paralysis?"

It is a question worth pondering today. The people in Jesus' day believed it was easier for a body to be healed than a soul to be forgiven. Do we believe that today, or do we believe it is easier for a person to be saved rather than be healed of some dreadful, life-threatening disease?

What do we do with the concept of wholeness? How might we deal more effectively with people who are sick, struggling, suffering, or incapacitated?

A
Application for Today

The people at one particular "old folks home" were not atypical of many in their situation. A number of them sat listless on sofas or in wheelchairs, seemingly existing only for the next mealtime. They engaged in little conversation with one another, and although they were quick to notice strangers who entered the room, they were reluctant to speak. And then, two students from a Christian college volunteered their services. They had *planned* to go to the home to teach a Bible study for those who might be interested. Few were. The students were determined to find out why, and they began to have personal conversations with those who sat in the lobby.

The students listened closely to what the residents told them about their before-the-home lives and also about life at the retirement center. Rather than have a Bible study, the students decided to host a weekly variety show to showcase the talents of some of the residents—a number of them had musical skills and several had the ability to recite poems they had learned in their youth. A few had good jokes to tell. Some were capable of leading a songfest. The students pre-interviewed one or two residents each week and created a "this is your life" presentation with visuals from days long gone and from audio portions of their interviews. The weekly Saturday afternoon show became a huge hit! At the close of each show, the students invited residents to their Bible study on Sunday afternoon. Not only did attendance pick up among the residents, but relatives of those who lived in the home began to attend. At the close of each Bible study, the students offered to pray with those who wanted prayer. Eventually, the students found themselves recruiting several of their college friends to join them in this ministry—nearly everyone who came to the show came to the study, and nearly everyone at the study wanted prayer! In the first six months, the students had the privilege of leading eight elderly residents of that home to a personal relationship with Jesus Christ, and of praying with eighteen of their relatives to receive Jesus as their Savior.

After two years of ministry there, the owner of the facility asked to meet with the students personally. He noted in his conversation with them that the medical condition of the residents had improved significantly in the time they had been involved at the home. He said, "I hear more laughter and less moaning. We are dispensing fewer pain medications because the people are asking for less pain medication. We have had fewer deaths per year in the last two years than in the previous ten years." The students knew that Jesus Christ was at work in the lives of the residents.

Who do you know who needs to be approached and helped as a whole person? How important is it to offer the physically sick an opportunity to accept Christ?

S
Supplementary Scriptures to Consider

Jesus not only healed sick bodies, but He restored those who were considered unclean on account of their ailments. Part of being made whole is being restored to one's family and community:

> Now a leper came to Him, imploring Him, kneeling down to Him and saying to Him, "If You are willing , You can make me clean."
>
> Then Jesus, moved with compassion, stretched out His hand and touched him, and said to him, "I am willing; be

> cleansed." As soon as He had spoken, immediately the leprosy left him, and he was cleansed. And He strictly warned him and sent him away at once, and said to him, "See that you say nothing to anyone; but go your way, show yourself to the priest, and offer for your cleansing those things which Moses commanded, as a testimony to them" (Mark 1:40–44).

- Jesus is not offended by our sin or sickness. He makes us clean. This is contrary to natural order. Dirt sullies the clean garment or object; clean items do not make the dirt or grime clean. Jesus had *cleansing* power. Is there anyone you would be afraid to touch physically? How important is touch to the healing process?

- Jesus admonished this leper to go to the priest. In that time and culture, Jews who were lepers had to be pronounced clean of their disease before they could mingle freely in society or return to synagogue services. Is there a prejudice today against sick people attending church services? To what extent does the Lord challenge us to reach out to the unclean people in our world today and share the gospel with them, including touching them as we pray for them?

Jesus did not follow man-made customs when it came to healing and delivering those in need:

> He entered the synagogue again, and a man was there who had a withered hand. So they watched Him closely, whether He would heal him on the Sabbath, so that they might accuse Him. And He said to the man who had the withered hand, "Step forward." Then He said to them, "Is it lawful on the Sabbath to do good or to do evil, to save life or to kill?" But they kept silent. And when He had looked around at them with anger, being grieved by the hardness of their hearts, He said to the man, "Stretch out your hand." And he stretched it out, and his hand was restored as whole as the other (Mark 3:1–5).

Is there ever a time when we should delay speaking a word of healing or encouragement to a person in need? Is it ever acceptable for us to allow any religious ritual or tradition to take precedence over helping an individual?

Jesus responded to all who reached out to receive what He offered, even if they came to Him secretly:

> Now a certain woman had a flow of blood for twelve years, and had suffered many things from many physicians. She had spent all that she had and was no better, but rather grew worse. When she heard about Jesus, she came behind Him in the crowd and touched His garment. For she said, "If only I may touch His clothes, I shall be made well."
>
> Immediately the fountain of her blood was dried up, and she felt in her body that she was healed of the affliction. And Jesus, immediately knowing in Himself that power had gone out of Him, turned around in the crowd and said, "Who touched My clothes?"

> But His disciples said to Him, "You see the multitude thronging You, and You say, 'Who touched Me?'"
>
> And He looked around to see her who had done this thing. But the woman, fearing and trembling, knowing what had happened to her, came and fell down before Him and told him the whole truth. And he said to her, "Daughter, your faith has made you well. Go in peace, and be healed of your affliction" (Mark 5:25–34).

- This woman touched Jesus with her faith. That is the way we touch Jesus today. How do *you* express faith to the Lord?

- This woman had been labeled as unclean and should not have been in a crowd of people. Part of her reluctance in speaking up no doubt was the fear others would not believe she had been healed. Can you identify with this fear? Have you ever felt reluctant to tell how Christ has made you whole because you didn't want others to know that you were ever *not* whole?

- Once healed, this woman was fully restored to her community. She could attend synagogue services and be part of family and community activities for the first time in twelve years. In what ways do we sometimes ostracize—perhaps unintentionally—those who are sick or impaired from participating in community or church activities? What might we do to make them feel more a part?

- Consider for a moment how you would have felt if you had been this woman and Jesus had demanded to know, "Who touched Me?" Are you ever reluctant to express to others the good things the Lord has done for you?

Word may have spread rapidly that a woman touched the hem of Jesus' garment and was healed. Mark tells us in the next chapter of his Gospel:

> When they had crossed over, they came to the land of Gennesaret and anchored there. And when they came out of the boat, immediately the people recognized Him, ran through that whole surrounding region, and began to carry about on beds those who were sick to wherever they heard He was. Wherever He entered, into villages, cities, or the country, they laid the sick in the marketplaces, and begged Him that they might just touch the hem of His garment. And as many as touched Him were made well. (Mark 6:53–56).

How does sharing what Jesus has done for us inspire others to believe Jesus can and will help them in their need? Can you cite a specific example in which the story of another person encouraged you in your faith? Has there been a time in which your sharing a personal healing experience encouraged another person to believe in God's power?

Jesus taught:

> "The Sabbath was made for man, and not man for the Sabbath. Therefore the Son of Man is also Lord of the Sabbath" (Mark 2:27–28).

What do these statements of Jesus mean to you? Do you keep the Sabbath—an entire day set apart to honor the Lord? To what extent does keeping the Sabbath help us find balance and wholeness in our lives?

- Do you ever put your spiritual life into a Sunday box and think of the remaining days as being *secular* days?

I
Introspection and Implications

4 ✓ 1. There's an old adage, "There's a time and place for everything." Would Jesus have held to this principle when it came to helping a person? Why or why not?
What about you?

5 ✓ 2. How reluctant are you to discuss spiritual matters with another person? Why?

6 ✓ 3. With whom do you relate most in the story of the paralytic man whom Jesus made whole: The four friends? The critical scribes? The amazed onlookers? The paralyzed man?

C
Communicating the Good News

Four of his friends brought the paralyzed man to Jesus. How important is it that we bind ourselves to friends who are of like faith and go as a group to help others in need? How much more effective is the witness of several people in sharing the gospel and God's plan of salvation?

If you are involved in a practical ministry of helping others today, is there a further spiritual dimension you might incorporate into that ministry? If you are involved today in a ministry that is primarily evangelistic, is there a practical dimension you might add to your ministry? Would these additional dimensions put you off purpose or create an enlarged purpose?

Lesson #3

JESUS COMMANDS NATURE

Command: to give orders that must be kept,
to gain control over something or someone
by personal power or authority

B
Bible Focus

> *On the same day, when evening had come, He said to them, "Let us cross over to the other side." Now when they had left the multitude, they took Him along in the boat as He was. And other little boats were also with Him. And a great windstorm arose, and the waves beat into the boat, so that it was already filling. But He was in the stern, asleep on a pillow. And they awoke Him and said to Him, "Teacher, do You not care that we are perishing?"*
>
> *Then He arose and rebuked the wind, and said to the sea, "Peace, be still!" And the wind ceased and there was a great calm. But He said to them, "Why are you so fearful? How is it that you have no faith?" And they feared exceedingly, and said to one another, "Who can this be, that even the wind and the sea obey Him!" (Mark 4:35–41)*

The Sea of Galilee is a small body of water, about twelve-and-a-half miles long and between four and seven-and-a-half miles wide. It is below sea level and is surrounded by mountains. As winds blow into the area from the Mediterranean Sea to the west, they can become intense. Moving rapidly down to the Sea of Galilee through various valleys and passes, the winds can take on a whipping quality—as if blender's blades are turned on high and then are suddenly thrust into a vat of water. Fierce storms can quickly arise on the Sea of Galilee.

What Jesus' disciples apparently forgot in the midst of this sudden storm was what He said at the outset of their journey, "Let us cross over to the other side." It was at His command that they had entered their boats and begun their journey. Everything Jesus had commanded thus far in their experience with Him had come to pass. They lost sight of this as the winds began to howl and churn the waters beneath them.

The truth is always: Where Jesus intends to go, He goes. What Jesus intends to accomplish, He accomplishes. If Jesus commands you to do something, He will ensure you are able to do it. There was absolutely no doubt in Jesus' mind He would arrive safely on the opposite shore that night. He climbed into the boat, went to sleep, and stayed asleep, even as the winds blew, the waves beat against the boat, and the boat began to take on water.

The disciples awoke Jesus and said, "Do You not care that we are perishing?" (Mark 4:38)

They had already concluded two things: one, they were on the verge of dying, and two, Jesus didn't care. They drew a conclusion about their fate that was untrue. They drew a conclusion about Jesus' compassion that was equally incorrect.

Jesus arose and spoke to the wind and to the sea. He rebuked what had *caused* the storm in the first place, and He spoke peace to the sea which was displaying the *effects* of the wind. He then turned and spoke to His disciples, asking, "Why are you so fearful? How is it that you have no faith?"

Storms arise in every person's life. Some are natural and material storms that are very real—they produce practical problems that threaten to destroy us physically, financially, or materially. Some are emotional or spiritual storms that are equally real—they create relational problems that threaten to destroy marriages, families, churches, and communities. The ultimate impact of storms, however, is that they nearly always divert us from what God has called us to do. Very few storms we experience are truly deadly—most illness are not terminal, most financial problems do not end in bankruptcy, most marital arguments do not lead to divorce, most runaway children find their way home, most depression lifts, most things we worry about do not come to pass. We need to see storms for what they are—temporary, inconvenient, fear-producing *opportunities* for our faith to be exercised and strengthened.

The Gospel of Mark makes it clear that Jesus—by whom and through whom all things were initially created—has absolute control over natural law. Jesus challenges us to trust Him to speak to the stormy winds—to rebuke the *cause* of our storm, and also to bring calm to the *effects* of the storm. We must also trust that Jesus cares enough to help us. Even when we know Jesus *can* right what is wrong, our greater struggle is often believing He cares enough about us personally to do so.

Do you see Jesus today as more powerful than whatever is coming against your life to hinder your effectiveness for Christ in this world?

Do you truly believe Jesus cares about what happens to you?

A
Application for Today

The man had been addicted to nicotine for twenty years—he was a two-pack-a-day smoker. He didn't *want* to be a cigarette smoker, however, and he expressed his desire to be free of the nicotine habit at a spiritual retreat he and his wife were attending. Several people at the retreat prayed for him to be set free from this addiction, and immediately, he lost all desire for nicotine! Even he was surprised at the disgust he suddenly felt toward the smell of cigarette smoke and the physical calm he continued to feel in the coming hours without any aid from nicotine.

However, it took fourteen months, for the man to get completely beyond the habit of reaching for a cigarette at times when he didn't know what to do with his hands or what to say in a conversation. He had been set free from his addiction, but still had to deal with reversing an ingrained habit.

The woman had been sick to the point she felt despair. The parasite she had contracted on an overseas trip had sapped her energy to the point she was virtually bedridden for a year. Discouraged that physicians were unable to diagnose her problem, and therefore, were unable to treat it, she began to question if she would ever feel good again. By her own admission, she began to act and speak about herself as if she would be an invalid for the rest of her life. Then, a specialist identified her problem and prescribed several courses of treatment. Slowly but surely, the parasites within her body's tissues were killed. She eventually was free of her disease, but she still faced the difficult task of rebuilding her strength. Equally difficult, again by her own admission, was the task of seeing herself as a person who was well.

We often fail to deal with *both* the cause and effects of trouble in our lives. We may deal with a physical component of an ailment but fail to deal with the emotional aspect. We may confront an addiction, but not address habits related to it. We might get out of debt, but fail to address the greed or the emotional need that drove us to spend more than we should have. We might treat symptoms, but never get to the root disease. We might lose weight, but fail to adopt good eating habits or address the emotional issues underlying our original weight gain.

The natural world has causes and effects—root disease and symptoms, core problems, and outer habits—and the good news is that Jesus addresses both! God governs the *whole* of His creation. He desires that we trust Him to deal with the entirety of any problem we face.

Is there an issue today you can't seem to resolve? Is there perhaps a hidden cause that hasn't been addressed?

Is there an irritating set of circumstances you can't seem to change? What is the underlying issue?

Does a problem keep recurring? Have you failed to address some of the secondary behaviors or habits that keep an issue from being fully resolved?

Ask the Lord to help you identify the root cause of the problem and all its effects. Trust Him to care enough about you to help you deal with the whole of the circumstance.

S

Supplementary Scriptures to Consider

Jesus not only had the power to calm the Sea of Galilee, He had the power to walk on it!

The Gospel of Mark says:

> Immediately He made His disciples get into the boat and go before Him to the other side, to Bethsaida, while He sent the

> multitude away. And when He had sent them away, He departed to the mountain to pray. Now when evening came, the boat was in the middle of the sea; and He was alone on the land. Then He saw them straining at rowing, for the wind was against them. Now about the fourth watch of the night He came to them, walking on the sea, and would have passed them by. And when they saw Him walking on the sea, they supposed it was a ghost, and cried out; for they all saw Him and were troubled. But immediately He talked with them and said to them, "Be of good cheer! It is I, do not be afraid." Then He went up into the boat to them, and the wind ceased. And they were greatly amazed in themselves beyond measure, and marveled (Mark 6:45–51).

- Nothing keeps Jesus from going where He desires to go. The same is true today. If Jesus commands you to take a particular action, He will equip, empower, and enable you to do what He commands. As the old saying goes, "Where He leads, He provides." Is there something today you believe the Lord is asking you to do? Are you struggling to determine how, when, where, and by what means? In what areas is your faith being challenged?

- Jesus came to His disciples in their time of need. His presence not only resolved their problem, but brought them comfort. Can you recall a time in your life when the Lord met a need in your life *and* comforted you with His presence? How does the Lord's miracle-working power and His comfort-giving presence work together? What does this say to you about the way we are to help others in need?

- Jesus needed the waters of the Sea of Galilee to be a surface to walk on, not to be a floating surface. So He made it so. He had the ability to use His creation for whatever purpose He desired. Is there a resource in your life today the Lord might desire for you to use differently? Is there something you own that you haven't been using fully that might have a second life? Is there a talent you have that the Lord might desire for you to redevelop and use in a new way?

A number of prophets in the Old Testament superceded natural law at various times, including the prophet Elisha:

> He [Elisha] took up the mantle of Elijah that had fallen from him, and went back and stood by the bank of the Jordan. Then he took the mantle of Elijah that had fallen from him, and struck the water, and said, "Where is the LORD God of Elijah?" And when he also had struck the water, it was divided this way and that; and Elisha crossed over (2 Kings 2:13–14).

- Was it any more difficult for Elisha to part waters and walk on dry ground, than for Jesus to walk on the water? In what very practical and normal ways do we use, work with, or handle natural resources today—the use of which would astound those who lived thousands of years ago? Are there ways in which God might inspire His people to unlock the still-secret ways spiritual power might impact natural resources?

- This miracle of parted waters was an answer to Elisha's question whether he had the same prophetic power that Elijah, his mentor, had displayed. How often do we wonder if we have the same power of God in our lives as someone else, or if we have as much spiritual authority or ability as another person we have admired or followed?

- There's no mention that Elisha ever again used Elijah's mantel to part the Jordan's waters. There's no mention that Jesus ever again walked on water. Virtually all the natural-law miracles in the Old Testament are one-time occurrences in Scripture. Why is it important to look at the reason and the effects of these miracles? What do they tell us about God's power? What do they tell us about God's ability to work through a person to change natural circumstances?

I
Introspection and Implications

1. Is there a problem you are facing that seems overwhelming to you? Do these miracles of Jesus encourage you? Why or why not?

2. When something seems to defy natural law today, do your thoughts turn first to God . . . or do you think first about some other “force” that might be at work? How important is it that we see God as the author of all natural law and the source of all natural provision? How important is it that we see God as absolutely in control of all aspects of His creation at all times?

3. Do you sometimes question whether God “loves you enough” or “cares enough about what happens to you” to act on your behalf? How does questioning God’s compassion, love, concern, or “care” limit, or even squelch, faith?

4. In what ways does fear keep us from believing that God can act and will act on our behalf? Is fear keeping you from trusting God in an area of your life today?
   Can you identify the nature of that fear? Very often when we identify *why* we are afraid—or *what* we fear most—we are set free to begin to believe God will provide what we need.

C
Communicating the Good News

The Roman believers lived in a world in which they were often threatened by Roman officials. How might the miracles of Jesus have comforted these believers who were living in stormy times? To what extent might recounting the miracles of Jesus comfort a person who is going through a tough time today?

Jesus said to His disciples when He came walking on water to them, "Be of good cheer! It is I, do not be afraid" (Mark 6:50). Can you recall a time you needed to be reminded to rejoice in your faith and not be afraid? In what ways might a person benefit from hearing your words of encouragement? How can you tell a person not to fear, or to have good cheer, and not sound as if you are dismissing the enormity of their problem?

LESSON #4

JESUS RAISES THE DEAD

Potential: the possibility or likelihood of future development, achievement, or fulfillment—the whole of what a person might be and do

B
Bible Focus

Behold, one of the rulers of the synagogue came, Jairus by name. And when he saw Him, he fell at His feet and begged Him earnestly, saying, "My little daughter lies at the point of death. Come and lay Your hands on her, that she may be healed, and she will live." So Jesus went with him, and a great multitude followed Him and thronged Him. . . .

While He was still speaking [to a woman with a flow of blood for twelve years], some came from the ruler of the synagogue's house who said, "Your daughter is dead. Why trouble the Teacher any further?"

As soon as Jesus heard the word that was spoken, He said to the ruler of the synagogue, "Do not be afraid; only believe." And He permitted no one to follow Him except Peter, James, and John the brother of James. Then He came to the house of the ruler of the synagogue, and saw a tumult and those who wept and wailed loudly. When He came in, He said to them, "Why make this commotion and weep? The child is not dead, but sleeping."

And they ridiculed Him. But when He had put them all outside, He took the father and the mother of the child, and those who were with Him, and entered where the child was lying. Then He took the child by the hand, and said to her, "Talitha, cumi," which is translated, "Little girl, I say to you, arise." Immediately the girl arose and walked, for she was twelve years of age. And they were overcome with great amazement. But He commanded them strictly that no one should know it, and said that something should be given her to eat" (Mark 5:22–24, 35–43).

All of us will die. But not all of us will die today. Jairus's daughter would one day die, but not on the day Jesus spoke to her, "Talitha, cumi"—"Little girl, I say to you, arise."

As believers in Christ Jesus, we have the hope that we live as long as God has a purpose for us to live on this earth. But, if we die as believers in Christ, we have the hope of eternity with our heavenly Father. Those who reject Christ will tragically spend eternity in hell, separated from God. Either way, we are alive and in relationship with our heavenly Father.

What was the purpose of this little girl living? Her story is actually told in conjunction with a story we dealt with in a previous lesson. It was while Jesus was on His way to Jairus's house that a woman with an issue of blood touched the hem of His garment and was instantly healed. Mark wrote specifically in his Gospel that this woman had an issue of blood for twelve years. He tells us specifically that Jairus's daughter was twelve years old.

The woman with the issue of blood had been slowly dying—and then was restored instantly to fullness of life. Jairus's little girl had been living, growing up as a normal girl—and then had suddenly died. Death and life. Life and death. Both are fully in God's hands. These stories make that abundantly clear.

But Jairus's little girl does not remain dead. In fact, Jesus regarded her as only sleeping.

In Jewish tradition, numbers have meaning, including the application of numbers to age. Twelve is a number associated with maturity, fullness, potential. It takes twelve years for a child to grow to maturity—twelve was the age at which boys were examined in the Law and qualified to be full members of the spiritual community. Twelve was traditionally the age at which a girl was considered to be a woman, capable of becoming betrothed and eventually bearing a child. Physical maturation was coupled with spiritual maturation—a twelve-year-old at Jesus' time was considered fully responsible for his or her own choices and behavior. Twelve was a number for the fulfillment of potential—all necessary elements were present for a person's life to take on a fullness of meaning and purpose.

The woman with the issue of blood had experienced a waning of her potential, her place in society, her purpose. Jesus restored these to her.

Jairus's daughter was on the cusp of becoming the woman God had created her to be—of displaying, experiencing, and realizing the fullness of meaning and purpose God had for her.

The enemy of our souls will always seek to rob us of fulfillment, meaning, and purpose. He will always try to diminish or deny our potential. Death is his final blow to our potential.

Jesus, in sharp contrast, by His healing and raising of these two women, gave the opportunity for fulfillment. He provides and encourages meaning and purpose. He upholds and extends opportunities for us to realize our potential.

Is something dying in you today? Do you feel you have lost some of what has given your life meaning? Is your sense of purpose and genuine satisfaction ebbing from your life? Trust Jesus to stop the hemorrhage of your potential and to restore you to a fullness of who you are and what you are to accomplish in your life.

Do you feel you are being held back, or stopped in some way, when you are on the brink of fulfilling the reason you are on the earth? Do you feel you are living in a dream-like haze of what might be, but isn't yet? Trust

Jesus to *awaken* you so you can live in the fullness of who He desires for you to be, and be able to engage fully in all things He desires for you to do.

A
Application for Today

They were sixty-seven-years old when they went to Africa, paying their own way, to work in an orphanage for children whose parents had died in a great plague. Their family members told them it was time to retire, not launch out on such a bold adventure. Their children feared for their parents' health and safety, and if truth be told, also for their loss of inheritance. What did this couple have to say in reply?

They sent a letter to their family and friends in which they wrote, "For years we have felt God wanted us to take care of orphan children. We adopted three children and raised them as well as we knew how. They are grown now and have children of their own. They love the Lord, have good jobs, and are making their own contribution to the world. We are proud of them, and recognize we must let them live their own lives fully.

"We both retired from jobs two years ago and in the last two years, we've sat and stared at each other from our living room rocking chairs. We've bemoaned the loss of feeling useful. We finally faced the fact that we were very dissatisfied with our present lives. We talked it over and we both still feel that God wants us to take care of orphan children. So that's what we are going to do. We have felt led to make a three-year commitment, and we are trusting God to give us the health, strength, ability, and resources to fulfill that commitment. We are hoping He will let us renew our pledge for many more years beyond that time. Since the day we decided to go to Africa and work in this orphanage, we both have felt a tremendous renewal of energy, purpose, strength, enthusiasm, and faith. We feel more alive than we've felt in ten years. We can hardly wait to go. Pray for us, but please do not try to stop us. We feel alive again!"

Death takes many forms.

Relationships can die. Talents can perish from lack of practice or use. Certain products can be replaced with new generations of products, and thus, job skills can cease to be useful. Companies can merge or go out of business. Careers can die for lack of pursuit or adaptation. Neighborhoods and machines can both die for lack of repair and maintenance. Societies can die for lack of morality.

Jesus comes to give life in every form that is godly.

Is there something today that is waning, dying, or diminishing in you? Is there something in a relationship, or in a group of people with whom you associate, that seems to be disappearing or decreasing more than it is developing or expanding? Do you still have a desire to *live*—grow, mature, develop, expand, use, participate, give, show love, contribute something useful? Then trust Jesus that His life-giving power will flow in that specific part of your being, your family, your church, and your city.

S
Supplementary Scriptures to Consider

In the case of Jairus's daughter, Jesus raised a little girl from her deathbed with only His closest disciples present. Another time, Jesus publicly restored a young person to life:

> Now it happened, the day after, that He went into a city called Nain; and many of His disciples went with Him, and a large crowd. And when He came near the gate of the city, behold, a dead man was being carried out, the only son of his mother; and she was a widow. And a large crowd from the city was with her. When the Lord saw her, He had compassion on her and said to her, "Do not weep." Then He came and touched the open coffin, and those who carried him stood still. And He said, "Young man, I say to you, arise." So he who was dead sat up and began to speak. And He presented him to this mother.
>
> Then fear came upon all, and they glorified God, saying, "A great prophet has risen up among us"; and, "God has visited His people." And this report about Him went throughout all Judea and all the surrounding region (Luke 7:11–17).

- Jesus again was demonstrating His power to give life over death. Death destroys life, but with Jesus, His life destroys death! Jesus reverses whatever comes against God's plan for your life. In the case of this young man in Nain, part of this son's purpose was to provide for his mother. Jesus called him awake to live out that purpose. What does this story say to you about the purpose God still has for your life?

- Jesus was *moved with compassion*. No one asked Jesus to intervene. He acted of His own volition. He stepped in, when nobody else did. His purpose in doing so was, in part, to reveal to those who were with Him that He was not afraid to confront death, or anything else that might diminish, destroy, or impair peoples' lives. He cared to the point He was willing to risk His own reputation and receive criticism for stopping a public funeral procession, even when no one asked Him to do so or gave Him prior permission to. Do you know someone today who is being shackled or harmed in some way? Do you know someone who is being abused? Do you have enough compassion to take action on that person's behalf?

Jesus said:

> "The thief does not come except to steal, and to kill, and to destroy. I have come that they may have life, and that they may have it more abundantly" (John 10:10).

- What things can the devil steal from a Christian? What things does he have power to kill (beyond the body)? What things does the devil take pleasure in destroying? In you? In your family? In the church?

- What does it mean to have a life that is *abundant*?

I
Introspection and Implications

1. How do you personally determine if something needs to be restored, or replaced?

2. Every living thing has a lifespan. Relationships are "living" entities. How do you determine if a relationship is dead and needs to be buried or if it still can be resuscitated and live in health? How do you determine if something you have pursued or valued—including a relationship or membership—is over, or just in need of renewal? (Don't think in terms of marriage alone, but also in terms of business partnerships and employment situations, friendships, club activities and memberships, and church committees.)

3. Do you feel you are living in the fullness of your potential? If not, what might you do? If so, what action can you take to help ensure that you will continue to experience maximum meaning, purpose, and satisfaction in your life? What steps can you take and satisfaction in your life? What steps can you take to ensure that you will remain productive and active as long as possible?

4. There's an old saying, "When you stop growing you start dying." Do you agree? Can you cite an example in your life in which you, somebody you know, or a business for which you worked, started "dying" when it stopped growing?

   In your personal life, what "growth opportunities" are you pursuing right now?

C
Communicating the Good News

How encouraging is it to share with a person the news that there's more to life than what he or she is currently experiencing and that the something more is something good? What specifically would you tell an unbeliever that Jesus desires to give to their life?

What specifically would you encourage a believer to trust Jesus to give so that person might experience genuine abundance?

Lesson #5

JESUS MULTIPLIES BREAD AND FISH

Bread: the staple of life, including all things that give meaning and purpose and satisfaction to life

B
Bible Focus

Then the apostles gathered to Jesus and told Him all things, both what they had done and what they had taught. And He said to them, "Come aside by yourselves to a deserted place and rest a while." For there were many coming and going, and they did not even have time to eat. So they departed to a deserted place in the boat by themselves.

But the multitudes saw them departing, and many knew Him and ran there on foot from all the cities. They arrived before them and came together to Him. And Jesus, when He came out, saw a great multitude and was moved with compassion for them, because they were like sheep not having a shepherd. So He began to teach them many things. When the day was now far spent, His disciples came to Him and said, "This is a deserted place, and already the hour is late. Send them away, that they may go into the surrounding country and villages and buy themselves bread; for they have nothing to eat."

But He answered and said to them, "You give them something to eat."

And they said to Him, "Shall we go and buy two hundred denarii worth of bread and give them something to eat?"

But He said to them, "How many loaves do you have? Go and see."

And when they found out they said, "Five, and two fish."

Then He commanded them to make them all sit down in groups on the green grass. So they sat down in ranks, in hundreds and in fifties. And when He had taken the five loaves and the two fish, He looked up to heaven, blessed and broke the loaves, and gave them to His disciples to set before them; and the two fish He divided among them all. So they all ate and were filled. And they took up twelve baskets full of fragments and of the fish. Now those who had eaten the loaves were about five thousand men (Mark 6:30–44).

The time of year in which this miracle took place was likely close to the Passover Feast, which was celebrated in the spring. Mark wrote that the people sat on *green* grass. The story deals with a large number of people—five thousand men, which may be translated to five thousand families.

Perhaps as many as twenty thousand people were gathered to hear Jesus and experience His ministry. A crowd that size would have only been likely during Passover. The area in which this miracle took place was on one of two main routes people would have taken to travel from northern Israel to Jerusalem, where the feast was centered.

The Passover Feast involved eating bread and lamb. It was a meal originally eaten under the stipulation that the Israelites be clothed and have on their sandals; in other words, be ready to move quickly when the signal was given. The feast was eaten in family groupings. It was the Israelites' last meal in Egyptian bondage before they embarked on a journey that led to their freedom and their full establishment as a nation.

Jesus was addressing people who were without—they were not poor slaves, necessarily, as the Israelites had been, but they had consumed all the food they had brought in their desire to stay and hear what Jesus had to say. In a crowd of thousands, only five loaves of bread and two small fish could be found in the food basket of one young boy. The feast Jesus provided involved bread and fish (the food of the area). He personally was the lamb, but the Lamb had not yet been slain. (See Revelation 13:8.)

The purpose of the Passover Feast was to remember a truth central to the Jewish faith: God provides what we need to get from bondage to freedom. He provides direction, nourishment for strength and energy, and the emotional bonds and practical support of family and friends.

In multiplying loaves and fishes to feed the five thousand, look at how and what Jesus did. He spent the day teaching, giving the people spiritual direction for their lives. His message called them away from their bondage to ritual and religion and toward the freedom of a spiritual relationship with their heavenly Father based on faith. Jesus provided ample provision, so much so that the disciples each had a full basket of food to eat after all the scraps had been collected. The people had been nourished both physically and spiritually, strengthened for their journey. They had been fed in well-ordered groups of fifty and a hundred people. Jesus' twelve disciples fed the masses, in a manner reminiscent of the twelve tribes of Israel being led by their respective elders.

What is the message to us today?

Jesus calls us to follow Him and in following, go from slavery to sin to freedom in serving. He gives us overall spiritual direction for our lives so we can follow Him all the way into eternity. By His Spirit, He gives us daily direction so we are able to make wise choices and decisions to live a productive and meaningful life day by day.

Jesus gives us total nourishment for our journey. He provides what we need spiritually and materially.

Jesus *groups* us into families and churches so we might encourage and build up one another, share spiritual gifts with one another, and work together to accomplish more together than we could accomplish alone.

Jesus takes what little we have, and multiplies it according to His infinite resources. He is our sufficiency—even more than sufficient—for every need we have and every challenge we face.

A
Application for Today

A little boy named Johnny knelt by his bed one night to say his prayers with his father and mother. As his father was tucking him into bed a few minutes later, Johnny asked, "Dad, lots of people are praying right now, aren't they?"

His father said, "You mean around the whole world?"

"Yes," Johnny said. "Lots and lots of prayers are going up, aren't they?"

"Well, yes," his father said. "I suppose there are. Thousands and thousands of prayers perhaps."

"How can God tell which one is mine?" Johnny asked.

The father sat on the edge of the bed for a moment and then replied, "Because God has a special 'Johnny receiver.' He knows just which prayer is yours."

Johnny looked a little puzzled. His father continued. "Lots of ideas come into your mind all day, don't they, son?" Dad asked.

"Sure," Johnny said. "Sometimes I can hardly keep up with all the ideas that fly through my head."

"Some of those ideas tell you, 'this is right, that is wrong' and some ideas say, 'this is good, that is bad,'" said Dad.

"Yes," Johnny said.

"Who do you supposed is giving you those ideas?" Dad asked.

"God?" Johnny replied.

"Right!" said Dad, and then he added, "And do you know how you can tell which of all those ideas is from God?"

"I have a God receiver!" Johnny said with a big grin.

Dad smiled back. "We can never figure out everything about God," Dad concluded, "but you can always know this. God has a receiver in His heart for hearing you, and you have a receiver in your heart for hearing God. The important thing is to keep the communication going."

How can God simultaneously hear and answer all the prayers at any given moment in time? How can He love all people personally and unconditionally?

How did Jesus multiply a few loaves and fish to feed thousands?

How does God multiply what we give to Him today?

How can Jesus provide full sufficiency for every believer, at all times, and in all ways? With our finite minds, we can never fully understand infinite power or any other aspect of infinity or eternity. Nevertheless, we each are given a measure of faith to believe God can take a little, multiply it, and produce much. He provides an overflowing abundance to each of us, so we might share the overflow with others.

S
Supplementary Scriptures to Consider

Jesus is not the first person in the Bible to multiply food. The prophet Elijah is associated with a provision-providing miracle:

> Then the word of the LORD came to him [Elijah], saying, "Arise, go to Zarephath, which belongs to Sidon, and dwell there. See, I have commanded a widow there to provide for you." So he rose and went to Zarephath. And when he came to the gate of the city, indeed a widow was there gathering sticks. And he called to her and said, "Please bring me a little water in a cup, that I may drink." And as she was going to get it, he called to her and said, "Please bring me a morsel of bread in your hand."
>
> So she said, "As the LORD your God lives, I do not have bread, only a handful of flour in a bin, and a little oil in a jar; and see, I am gathering a couple of sticks that I may go in and prepare it for myself and my son, that we may eat it, and die."
>
> And Elijah said to her, "Do not fear; go and do as you have said, but make me a small cake from it first, and bring it to me; and afterward make some for yourself and your son. For thus says the LORD God of Israel: 'The bin of flour shall not be used up, nor shall the jar of oil run dry, until the day the LORD sends rain on the earth.'"
>
> So she went away and did according to the word of Elijah, and she and he and her household ate for many days. The bin of flour was not used up, nor did the jar of oil run dry, according to the word of the LORD which He spoke by Elijah (1 Kings 17:8–16).

- One of life's basic needs is food, and one of life's greatest fears occurs when there is insufficient food. Millions of people around the world are just one or two meals away from starvation. How important is it that we trust God for our provision one meal at a time?

- With her flour and oil nearly gone, the widow of Zarephath very likely did *not* have faith to believe in making a thousand meals from what remained. But she apparently did have the faith to believe in *just one more meal*," and she did so each day for nearly three-and-a-half years until the rain finally returned to the skies. How important is it for us to recognize that God provides for us in an ongoing way as we continue to trust Him day-by-day-by-day? What happens to our faith and our sense of utter dependency on the Lord when we have far more than we need?

The prophet Elisha is also associated with a miracle involving multiplication of food:

> Then a man came from Baal Shalisha, and brought the man of God [Elisha] bread of the firstfruits, twenty loaves of barley bread, and newly ripened grain in his knapsack. And he [Elisha] said, "Give it to the people, that they may eat."
>
> But his servant said, "What? Shall I set this before one hundred men?"

> He said again, "Give it to the people that they may eat; for thus says the LORD: 'They shall eat and have some left over.'" So he set it before them; and they ate and had some left over, according to the word of the LORD (2 Kings 4:42–44).

Even in the face of this servant's doubt, God provided with *some left over.* The implication is that both Elisha and the doubting servant had enough to eat. Anytime we give to others what God has blessed, we will have sufficiency in our own lives. Have you ever felt God leading you to give, but you hoarded instead out of fear that you might not have enough for your family and yourself if you gave what God requested you give? What happened? Have you ever given as the Lord led you to give, even if you feared not having enough? What happened?

I
Introspection and Implications

1. What do you fear most about giving generously or extravagantly?

2. How important is it to give what the Lord directs us to give, and not merely what we think is affordable to give? What is your criterion for determining how *much* the Lord is asking you to give?

3. The widow of Zarephath was not an Israelite. The people Elisha fed were *"sons of the prophets"*—in our terms today, we might call them seminary or Bible-school students. The people whom Jesus fed represented a diverse group of Jewish people, with varying degrees of faith. None of us today can give our *"loaves and fishes"* directly to Jesus. Is it important to whom we give? What is your criterion for determining to whom to give?

4. What do you need most today? The miracle of multiplication shows us how Jesus met the people's needs spiritually, including their longing to be in deeper relationship with their heavenly Father. It shows how He met their physical need for strength and energy. It shows how He provided for them to eat in fellowship with a group. In all, their spiritual, physical, and emotional needs were met. In what area do you need a miracle of multiplication today?

5. Jesus did not create bread and fish from nothing—but rather from bits of bread and fish. Elijah's widow made cakes from bits of flour and oil. Elisha fed a hundred men from what amounted to bits of grain and bites of barley bread. In light of the need you have noted above, what might you give the Lord today with faith that He can and will multiply that to meet your total need? How do you respond to the concept that "like is multiplied into like"?

C
Communicating the Good News

What is the importance of meeting the practical, basic needs of people prior to giving them the gospel? How important is it to give a person a fish so that on a full stomach, that person can be taught *how* to fish?

Lesson #6

JESUS CONFRONTS HIS OPPOSITION

Self-defense: telling the untold truth about yourself to those who either don't know the truth or have swallowed a lie about you

B
Bible Focus

Then He began to speak to them in parables: "A man planted a vineyard and set a hedge around it, dug a place for the wine vat and built a tower. And he leased it to vinedressers and went into a far country. Now at vintage-time he sent a servant to the vinedressers, that he might receive some of the fruit of the vineyard from the vinedressers. And they took him and beat him and sent him away empty-handed. Again he sent them another servant, and at him they threw stones, wounded him in the head, and sent him away shamefully treated. And again he sent another, and him they killed; and many others, beating some, and killing some. Therefore still having one son, his beloved, he also sent him to them last, saying, 'They will respect my son.' But those vinedressers said among themselves, 'This is the heir. Come, let us kill him, and the inheritance will be ours.' So they took him and killed him and cast him out of the vineyard.

Therefore what will the owner of the vineyard do? He will come and destroy the vinedressers, and give the vineyard to others. Have you not even read this Scripture:

'The stone which the builders rejected
Has become the chief cornerstone.
This was the LORD's doing.
And it is marvelous in our eyes'?"

And they sought to lay hands on Him, but feared the multitude, for they knew He had spoken the parable against them. So they left Him and went away (Mark 12:1–12).

Jesus knew He had opposition. How could He forget? If you read the four Gospel accounts with an eye toward Jesus' opposition, you'll find it at almost every bend in the road He walked. The religious leaders displayed vast amounts of skepticism, jealousy, anger, and resentment toward Jesus, almost from the beginning of His public ministry. They attempted repeatedly to trick Him publicly into saying and doing things they hoped would bring disfavor from the masses, or that they might hold up for further ridicule. The religious leaders in the highest ranks of authority were threatened to their core by His power and popularity, and puzzled by His methods and His concepts.

Jesus didn't coddle those who opposed Him in hopes of softening their criticism or winning their favor through appeasement. He never backed away from who He was. Jesus never soft-pedaled the truth He taught. Whenever given an honest opportunity, He replied to His critics' questions and arguments boldly, directly, and decisively.

At the same time, Jesus didn't go out looking for a fight with His critics. He didn't say things specifically to taunt them. He didn't organize His followers to defeat them, although Jesus did warn His followers about their false teachings and hypocrisy.

The opponents in the incident above were the chief priests, scribes, and elders associated with the temple in Jerusalem. These were religious leaders of influence. They were the ones who accepted the sacrifices from the people and who governed the rituals of the religion, pronouncing some people welcome in the synagogues and prohibiting others from worship. Jesus saw no advantage to calling them names or openly criticizing them. As all the people sat listening to Him as He taught in the open teaching areas of the temple, Jesus told a story the leaders knew was about them.

The point of the parable was clear: "Reject Me if you will, but I will not cease to be important because you reject Me. In fact, I will become the cornerstone of something far greater. Why? Because I'm doing what God has sent Me to do."

What a marvelous message and example this is to us today.

We have a clear directive for how to deal with those who criticize us for our faith: If they ask questions or demand an explanation, we should be bold in answering and providing truth. Otherwise, we are wise to ignore them and move forward. We are not called to spend inordinate amounts of time currying favor or attempting to win their approval. We are never to go out in search of a conflict.

Never let criticism distract you from what the Lord is leading you to do.

A
Application for Today

The two men walked into the village and were immediately recognized as strangers. Two leaders of the town came to question where they were from and why they had come. The strangers said they had come with good news and asked to be given an opportunity to share it. The leaders agreed to give them an opportunity to speak and word spread quickly that the strangers were going to be speaking at the town hall that night.

The men were encouraged. The town had a reputation for being closed to strangers and highly skeptical of new ideas.

About half the people in the village liked what they heard. They wanted to hear more. They asked that the town hall be open the following night so the strangers could speak again.

The other half of the village didn't like anything they heard. They thought the message was far-fetched, a threat to their way of life, and that the men were dangerous. They asked that the men be sent away from the town and never be permitted to return.

The leaders of the village agreed to give the strangers one more night to tell their message, but after that, the strangers needed to leave. The strangers agreed; in fact, they didn't even ask for additional favor.

That night, half of the village entered the town hall boldly, eager to hear what the strangers might say. The other half of the village gathered outside the town hall, surrounding it and shouting taunts in loud and angry voices.

One of the strangers spoke earnestly and directly to those present, seemingly ignoring the crowd outside. The other stranger seemed distracted and concerned the crowd outside might become violent.

At the close of the meeting, many of those who had attended came to greet the strangers personally, and with tears in their eyes, thanked them for sharing their message.

The strangers left the village after the meeting was over, but not before one of them was punched in the eye and a large bucket of garbage was hurled in their direction.

One of the strangers left the village very encouraged: "Half the people wanted to hear us a second night! We had an opportunity to speak for a total of six-and-a-half hours to half of the town's population!"

The other stranger left the village discouraged: "I'll never do this again. We should have listened to what people told us about that village. We were poorly treated and had garbage thrown at us. It was dangerous. Nothing good could possibly take root in that village."

Would you have gone to that village? Would you have agreed to stay a second night, knowing half the town didn't want you around? How would you have evaluated your success?

Have you ever been so discouraged about how you were treated—or by the way in which your words or motives were misunderstood—that you felt like giving up completely in your efforts to share the gospel with other people?

Why is it important to be bold in what you say and then, to move on quickly if your message is not received?

Why must we refuse to become discouraged when we face opposition?

S
Supplementary Scriptures to Consider

After He was arrested in the Garden of Gethsemane, Jesus first faced the accusations of the Jewish religious leaders in Jerusalem:

> The high priest stood up in the midst and asked Jesus, saying, "Do you answer nothing? What is it these men testify against You?" But He kept silent and answered nothing.
>
> Again the high priest asked Him, saying to Him, "Are You the Christ, the Son of the Blessed?"
>
> Jesus said, "I am. And you will see the Son of Man sitting at the right hand of the Power, and coming with the clouds of heaven" (Mark 14:60-62).

When asked if He was the Christ, Jesus said, "Yes." If people ask you if you are a Christian, what do you say?" Do you try first to determine why they are asking, or if they believe in Christ?

Jesus was led by His accusers to Pilate, the governor (procurator) of Judea. The Jews at that time had no authority to enforce capital punishment; only Pilate could authorize a death sentence.

> Pilate asked Him, saying, "Are You the King of the Jews?" He answered him and said, "It is as you say" (Luke 23:3).

When people identify you as a leader, or attempt to recognize you for something good you have done, do you own up to your leadership skills and graciously receive their appreciation, or do you attempt to downplay your role or contribution? How does pride differ from honest self-appraisal? Why is it important to be true to ourselves so other people might feel free to be who they are? In what ways can a person devalue the worth of another person by downplaying their compliment?

Jesus was also brought before Herod, the figurehead "king of the Jews."

> Now when Herod saw Jesus, he was exceedingly glad; for he had desired for a long time to see Him, because he had heard many things about Him, and he hoped to see some miracle done by Him. Then he questioned Him with many words, but He answered him nothing (Luke 23:8–9).

Why is it better to ignore those who want to use us for their own amusement or advancement, rather than reply or cooperate with their request?

Jesus taught the Holy Spirit would give His followers guidance about what to say before religious and secular leaders:

> "Now when they bring you to the synagogues and magistrates and authorities, do not worry about how or what you should answer, or what you should say. For the Holy Spirit will teach you in that very hour what you ought to say" (Luke 12:11–12).

- Why is it important to rely on the Holy Spirit to teach us what to say, rather than to jump in on the basis of our human wisdom and knowledge and say what we *feel* like saying in the heat of the moment?

- Why is it important in most situations to avoid self-justification?

I
Introspection and Implications

1. A dilemma we often face is when to speak up and when to stay silent. What is your criterion for deciding when you should stand firm or speak, and when you should walk away or remain silent?

2. Tone of voice is important in dealing with one's critics and opponents. Two long passages in the New Testament tell us that Jesus spoke openly in terms of *"woe"* to the Pharisees, lawyers and other religious leaders.

   Read Luke 11:37–53 and Luke 12:1–3.

   Read Matthew 23:1–36.

   Jesus repeatedly used the word "woe" in speaking to the scribes, Pharisees, and lawyers. This word, however, was generally spoken in a tone indicating deep sorrow, not anger. What difference does it make as you read these passages to hear sorrow in Jesus' voice, rather than frustration or anger? Can you cite an example in your own life—either as a speaker or listener—when tone of voice made all the difference in the way a message was communicated?

3. Have you ever felt like a wimp for not taking a stand? Have you ever felt stupid for saying something when you should have kept quiet? How do you get beyond the residual feelings associated with your memories of such experiences?

4. How do you feel about people who seem to change their identity or their personality depending upon the circumstances in which they find themselves? Can you really trust such a person?

5. What do people tend to think of people who cower in the face of opposition?
How important was it for the Roman believers to know that Jesus did not change His message, or alter His identity, even in face-to-face confrontation with those who were opposed to everything He was, said, and did?

C
Communicating the Good News

Jesus gave clear directives as He sent His disciples out with the good news:

> Then He called His twelve disciples together and gave them power and authority over all demons, and to cure diseases. He sent them to preach the kingdom of God and to heal the sick. And He said to them, "Take nothing for the journey, neither staffs nor bag nor bread nor money; and do not have two tunics apiece.
>
> Whatever house you enter, stay there, and from there depart. And whoever will not receive you, when you go out of that city, shake off the very dust from your feet as a testimony against them.
>
> So they departed and went through the towns, preaching the gospel and healing everywhere (Luke 9:1–6).

How important is it to work with another person in ministry and to have a commitment to encourage and support each other? How important is it to have a prayer partner? How important is it to have someone who will be totally honest with you and hold you accountable for your behavior?

To *shake off the very dust from your feet* meant to give no thought to those who reject you. So many people today harbor deep feelings of rejection. They would rather hold on to them than let go and move on into tomorrow! Do you need to shake off the memory of a bad experience in your past so you can move forward freely and boldly in your Christian witness?

Lesson #7

JESUS DIES AND RISES FROM DEATH

Atonement: reconciliation, at-one-ment.
Atoning Sacrifice: a sacrifice requiring the shedding of blood that reconciles sinful man to Holy God—the death of Jesus on the Cross of Calvary

B
Bible Focus

He began to teach them that the Son of Man must suffer many things, and be rejected by the elders and chief priests and scribes, and be killed, and after three days rise again. He spoke this word openly (Mark 8:31–32).

Then they departed from there and passed through Galilee, and He did not want anyone to know it. For He taught His disciples and said to them, "The Son of Man is being betrayed into the hands of men, and they will kill Him. And after He is killed, He will rise the third day." But they did not understand this saying, and were afraid to ask Him (Mark 9:30–32).

Now they were on the road, going up to Jerusalem, and Jesus was going before them; and they were amazed. And as they followed they were afraid. Then He took the twelve aside again and began to tell them the things that would happen to Him: "Behold, we are going up to Jerusalem, and the Son of Man will be betrayed to the chief priests and to the scribes; and they will condemn Him to death and deliver Him to the Gentiles; and they will mock Him, and scourge Him, and spit on Him, and kill Him. And the third day He will rise again" (Mark 10:32–34).

Three times Jesus foretold He would suffer, die, and rise again after three days. The crucifixion and resurrection of Jesus should not have been a surprise to His closest followers, but they were.

Events unfolded precisely as Jesus said they would.

Jesus' disciples showed no evidence they really understood what He was saying. They were not unlike many of us today who, in the face of impending and certain conclusions, either

- Live in denial of reality
- Fear an impending reality to the point of paralysis
- Are overwhelmed with the enormity of the reality to the point of despair

Many people today know with their minds, but refuse to face fully these three facts:

- *Death is inevitable.* Many people die without resolving their affairs legally. They refuse to discuss death. Many are so fearful of death they cannot bear the thought of going to a cemetery or a funeral. Many who are facing death become deeply depressed.

- *Judgment after death is inevitable.* Many people live in denial that the Bible clearly presents two futures—one involving paradise and eternal life, the other involving torment and eternal death. Many people fear going to hell, but do nothing to ensure they will go to heaven. Others hope they will go to heaven but do nothing to ensure they don't go to hell.

- *Opposition to righteous behavior is inevitable.* Many people seem to believe if they do the right thing, they will glide through life without any criticism or rejection. Others try to ride an invisible fence—doing just enough good things to be liked by good people, and doing just enough bad things to avoid persecution from evil people. Others throw themselves a pity party when people don't applaud their relationship with Christ Jesus.

We need to get real about the inevitable!

This does not mean we need to be morbid or downcast. It does mean we should live in the truth and walk in the light of truth. We must fully engage in life, even as we prepare for death. We must confront our fears with faith, and choose to live with joy and hope.

The good news for the disciples of Jesus and for us is twofold. First, Jesus died a sacrificial atoning death so we might experience forgiveness of sins and receive the gift of eternal life. Without Jesus dying on the cross, we would still be bound by sin and guilt today. Praise God He died for you and me!

Second, Jesus rose from the dead. His resurrection is the seal on our hope of eternal life. Without Jesus rising from the dead, we would have no evidence for our belief that what Jesus said He would give us is something He *can* and *will* actually provide! Praise God that Jesus rose from death and lives forever at the right hand of our heavenly Father!

Jesus was not the only person to raise others from death. The prophets Elijah and Elisha did the same. Jesus was and is the only person ever to experience resurrection in this life. Resurrection means God brought Him back to life, by His divine power. Because Jesus lives, we can and do live. Our life in Him is unending. Death is but a transition moment from this earthly reality to the heavenly reality, from this finite world to the infinite glories of heaven, from this present age to eternity with God our Father.

What does it mean to you personally that Jesus died as an atoning sacrifice for you?

What does it mean to you personally that Jesus overcame the grave and rose from death?

A
Application for Today

Every major city of the world, most small cities, and many villages and rural areas have one thing in common: cemeteries.

Some people avoid going to a cemetery. They find it depressing and morbid.

Still others believe it is important to go to a cemetery occasionally—it's a sobering reminder they are going to be there one day.

Some people find value in visiting a cemetery periodically—it's a way they honor the memory of a person they love.

Some people see no value in visiting a cemetery—they hold to the opinion their loved one really isn't there, only a husk or shell their loved one once occupied.

Others find great comfort in visiting the grave of a loved one—it gives them a feeling of closeness to a person who was important to them.

Some people can't help but visit a cemetery—it's in the garden adjacent to the church they attend every Sunday. It is as familiar a place to them as any other building or park in town. They've almost lost the awareness that a cemetery is associated with death.

What about you? Do you relate to any of these responses? Would it make any difference if you did not know where your loved ones were buried or where you might one day be buried?

At least two places in Jerusalem lay claim to be the place where Jesus was crucified, died, buried, and rose from the grave. What is known with certainty about both places is that no body has ever been found in either tomb! There is no cemetery to visit to honor the memory of Jesus because He is still alive. We as Christians often take that fact for granted to the point that we lose sight of this truth: Jesus is the *only* person who has ever lived on this earth whose physical remains are not on this earth somewhere. (The only other exceptions are Enoch in the Old Testament, who "walked with God." See Genesis 5:24 and Elijah who was taken up in a heavenly chariot. See 2 Kings 2:11.) Overcoming death and the grave is the ultimate power Jesus displayed. It is a sign of His divinity that He so incarnated human flesh He took His glorified body with Him when He ascended to heaven.

MARTYR - A person who is killed or who suffers greatly for a religious cause (Merriam Webster Dict.)

S

Supplementary Scriptures to Consider

A significant number of people hold to the belief that Jesus was a martyr—that He was killed because He was a good man who taught good things and did good deeds. Jesus made it clear He was not a martyr:

> I lay down My life that I may take it again. No one takes it from Me, but I lay it down of Myself. I have power to lay it down, and I have power to take it again. This command I have received from My Father" (John 10:17–18).

- Why is it important that Jesus *chose* to die on the cross? How does saying *"I lay down My life that I may take it again"* differ from committing suicide?

- Why is it important that Jesus always related information about His death with information related to His resurrection?

Death w/out resurrection is just that; death.
Resurrection cannot happen w/out death.

When Jesus first spoke openly to His disciples about His impending suffering and death, Peter didn't like what he heard!

> Then Peter took Him aside and began to rebuke Him. But when He had turned around and looked at His disciples, He rebuked Peter, saying, "Get behind Me, Satan! For you are

> not mindful of the things of God, but the things of men" (Mark 8:32–33).

The word *Satan* means *accuser, adversary, enemy*. It refers to a person standing in opposition to God's plan. The devil is our ultimate accuser, adversary, and enemy, and the word *Satan* has come to be associated primarily with the devil. Jesus, however, was not calling Peter the devil. He was stating Peter's rebuke was in direct opposition to God's plan. Peter was speaking out of human wisdom and according to human desire, not God's will and desire. Jesus also saw the hand of the devil in using Peter to try and thwart Jesus's mission. Have you ever been tempted to talk someone into doing something you wanted them to do, only to discover it was not something God wanted for them or for you? Why is it critically important at all times to seek to put our lives into the center of God's plan, rather than ask God to indwell our human plans?

I
Introspection and Implications

1. Reflect upon this statement: We don't like talking about death because we haven't thought enough about heaven. How do your ideas about heaven impact your ideas about death?

2. Is there anything about "God's will" or "God's plan" for your life that frightens you? Why? How do you believe the Lord desires for you to confront that fear with faith?

3. For a Christian, is there always a good-news side to a bad-news story?

Ro 8:28
8!

4. Do you live in denial about anything? Do you worry a great deal about things you cannot control? Do you feel optimistic or pessimistic about your future? If your answer is "yes" to any of these questions, what do you believe the Lord desires for you?

5. What is your innermost "feeling" in response to the phrase "crucified and risen Lord"?

C
Communicating the Good News

The death and resurrection of Jesus Christ has always been the cornerstone of the gospel. When you tell others about Jesus, do you place first priority on sharing news of His death and resurrection? Why or why not? How important is it for others to hear and understand that Jesus Christ died a sacrificial death for their sins and rose from the grave so they might have hope of eternity with God their heavenly Father?

Notes to Leaders of Small Groups

As the leader of a small discussion group, think of yourself as a facilitator with three main roles:

- Get the discussion started
- Involve every person in the group
- Encourage an open, candid discussion that remains focused on the Bible

You certainly don't need to be the person with all the answers! Your success will be measured by how frequently and candidly you get others to share. In truth, much of your role is to ask questions, such as:

- What impacted you most in this lesson?
- What part of the lesson did you find troubling?
- What part of the lesson was encouraging or insightful?
- What part of the lesson would you like to explore further?

Express to the group at the outset of your study that your goal as a group is to gain new insights into God's Word—this is not the forum for defending a point of doctrine or a theological opinion. Stay focused on what God's Word says and means. The purpose of the study is also to share insights of how to apply God's Word to everyday life. *Every* person in the group can and should contribute—the collective wisdom that flows from Bible-focused discussion is often very rich and deep.

Seek to create an environment in which every member of the group feels free to ask questions of other members to gain greater understanding. Encourage group members to voice their appreciation to one another for new insights gained, and to be supportive of one another personally. Take the lead in doing this. Genuinely appreciate and value the contributions each person makes.

You may want to begin each study by having one or more members of the group read through the section provided under "Bible Focus." Ask the group specifically if it desires to discuss any of the questions under the "Application for Today" section, the "Supplemental Scriptures to Consider" section, the "Introspection and Implications" and "Communicating the Good News" section. You do not need to come to a definitive conclusion or consensus about any question asked in this study. Rather, encourage your group if it does not have a satisfactory Bible-based answer to a question to engage in further asking, seeking, and knocking strategies to discover the answers. Remember the words of Jesus: "Ask, and it will be given to you; seek, and you will find; knock, and it will be opened to you. For everyone who asks receives, and he who seeks finds, and to him who knocks it will be opened" (Matthew 7:7–8).

Finally, open and close your study with prayer. Ask the Holy Spirit, whom Jesus called the Spirit of Truth, to guide your discussion and to reveal what is of eternal benefit to you individually and as a group. As you close your time together, ask the Holy Spirit to seal to your remembrance what you have read and studied, and to show you ways in the upcoming days, weeks, and months how to apply what you have studied to your daily life and relationships.

General Themes for the Lessons

Each lesson in this study has one or more core themes. Continually pull the group back to these themes. You can do this by asking simple questions, such as, "How does that relate to ________?", "How does that help us better understand the concept of ________?", or "In what ways does that help us apply the principle of ________?"

A summary of general themes or concepts in each lesson follows:

Lesson #1

JESUS DELIVERS FROM UNCLEAN SPIRITS

Unclean spirits or demons—their existence and their limitations

Jesus' power over the entire spiritual realm

Lesson #2

JESUS FORGIVES AND HEALS

Wholeness

The link between forgiveness and healing

Healing and restoration

Lesson #3

JESUS COMMANDS NATURE

The wisdom of confronting both the causes and effects of problems

Believing God cares enough to act on your behalf

Lesson #4

JESUS RAISES THE DEAD

Our God-given potential

God's help for us as we seek to fulfill our potential

Types of death that are not physical

The abundant life

Jesus' desire to give us life

Lesson #5

JESUS MULTIPLIES BREAD AND FISH

God's provision for us:

His provision of spiritual direction, which leads us from bondage to freedom

His provision of nourishment that provides energy and strength for this life

His provision of human relationships that give us support and encouragement

The sufficiency of Jesus Christ in all areas of life

Lesson #6

JESUS CONFRONTS HIS OPPOSITION

Dealing with opposition in a manner that honors Christ

How and when to act or speak and when not to act or speak

Lesson #7

JESUS DIES AND RISES FROM DEATH

Atonement

Sacrificial death

Resurrection hope

Facing life's realities

NOTES

NOTES

NOTES

NOTES

NOTES

NOTES

NOTES